Altogether Enchanting

Sometimes designers are inspired to creativity by yarn textures, fibers and colors. I felt this inspiration when I was introduced to the owner of Aslan Trends Yarn Company and saw their beautiful yarn line.

Naturally, when asked to do a book of designs for them, I agreed, brimming with ideas and excitement. The colors and textures of the yarns generated images for me of gardens, seasons, flowers, leaves, of styles and shapes and of the word "enchantment".

As in all of my books, I try to design unique but functional, wearable pieces. Embellishments (easier than they look, I promise!) often enhance and add a special touch to the designs. My goal, knitters, is for you to get this response from all your friends, "Oh my, did you knit that? It's gorgeous!"

So, happy Aslan Trends knitting, and I hope you'll find inspiration and enchantment in these designs.

Nicky Epstein

*To Theresa
Happy knitting!
Nicky Epstein
6/12/10*

The Designs

SPELLBOUND WOVEN VESTLET
Page 4

CAPTIVATING CAPELET
Page 8

ROMANTIC AUTUMN PULLOVER
Page 10

COZY CABLE COAT
Page 14

BEWITCHING HOODED SCARF
Page 18

SPELLBOUND WOVEN VESTLET

SPELLBOUND WOVEN VESTLET

Made with Del Cerro, this unique piece is knit using a baby cable rib pattern worked in strips to make the woven bodice. If you are shy, the strips can be sewn closed. The front and back are the same and overlapped at each side edge with a stunning cord closure.

SIZES: SMALL/MEDIUM (LARGE/X-LARGE)

FINISHED MEASUREMENTS
Bust (unstretched): 38 (44)"/96.5 (111.5)cm
Bust (stretched): 42 (48)"/106 (122)cm

MATERIALS
*10 (11) 1¾oz/50g skeins (each approx 127yds/115m) of Aslan Trends Del Cerro (100% merino wool) in #0020 khaki
*Size 7 (4.5mm) knitting needles, OR SIZE NEEDED TO OBTAIN GAUGE
*Stitch holders or waste yarn
*Straight pins
*Tapestry needle
*Four JHB ¾"/2cm leatherall buttons #60325 (www.buttons.com)

GAUGE
29 sts and 23 rows = 4"/10cm over baby cable pattern (unstretched). TAKE TIME TO CHECK GAUGE.

Pattern Stitch
Baby Cable Pattern (multiple of 4 sts plus 2)
Rows 1 and 3 (WS) K2, *p2, k2; rep from *.
Row 2 P2, *K2, p2; rep from *.
Row 4 P2, *K2tog but leave on needle, insert right-hand needle between the 2 sts just knitted together and knit the first st again, then sl both sts from needle together; p2;

rep from *.
Rep Rows 1–4 for pattern.

Right Front
Cast on 66 (78) sts.
Rep Rows 1–4 of Baby Cable Pattern until piece measures 7 (8)"/18 (20.5)cm from beg, end with pattern Row 4.

Divide for Weaving Strips:

Strip 1
Next row (RS) Work 22 (26) sts in baby cable pattern for first strip, place rem 44 (52) sts on holder.
Continue even in pattern on these 22 (26) sts for 13 (14)"/33 (35.5)cm, end with pattern Row 4.
Place sts on a separate holder and cut yarn.

Strip 2
Slip next 22 (26) sts from first holder onto needle for second strip.
Continue in pattern on these 22 (26) sts for 14 (15)"/35.5 (38) cm, end with pattern Row 4.
Place sts on a separate holder and cut yarn.

Strip 3
Slip rem 22 (26) sts from first holder onto needle for third strip. Continue even in pattern on these 22 (26) sts for 15 (16)"/38 (40.5)cm, end with a RS row.

Joining Row (WS) Work 22 (26) sts of strip 3 in pattern; place sts of center strip 2 on needle and work these 22 (26) sts in pattern; work 22 (26) sts of strip 1 in pattern—66 (78) sts.
Continue in pattern for 5"/12.5cm. Bind off in pattern for shoulder.

Left Front
Work same as right front to joining row, reversing lengths of first and last strips.
Note: Place sts of Strip 3 on a holder for easier weaving.

Weaving
With RS facing, and cast-on edges at bottom, lay left front across right front. Place all three sections of left front on separate holders. With RS facing, starting with the longest strip on the left front, weave over, under, and over the three strips on right front and pin in place. Weave the center strip on left front, under, over, and under the three strips on right front and pin in place. Weave the last strip same as the first strip. Adjust the position of the strips if necessary to create a tight basketweave as pictured. With WS facing, stitch strips in place.
Place sts from all three strips onto needle and join. Starting with a WS row, complete same as right front.

Back
Work same as right front and left front.

Sleeves
Cast on 22 sts.
Rep Rows 1–4 of Baby Cable Pattern until piece measures about 12 (13)"/30.5 (33)cm. Bind off in pattern.

Finishing
Sew shoulder seams. Sew sleeves into armholes. Tack front and back together at corner side seams at cast-on edge for desired fit.

Side Closures (make 2)
I-cord (see Techniques section, page 55): Cast on 3 sts. *K3 sts. Do not turn work. Slide sts to right end of needle. Pull yarn to tighten. Rep from * for desired length approx 24"/61cm. Do not bind off the sts; leave them on a holder so length can be added or subtracted as needed. Loop cord around itself forming the serpent (following diagram) and two buttonloops. Use T-pins to anchor beginning with the cast-on edge and Kitchener st to join cast-on end to live sts of cord. Secure to sides of piece as pictured. Sew on buttons.

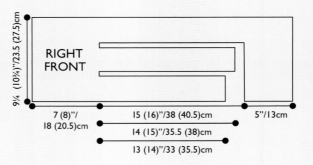

9¼ (10¾)"/23.5 (27.5)cm

RIGHT FRONT

7 (8)"/ 18 (20.5)cm

15 (16)"/38 (40.5)cm

5"/13cm

14 (15)"/35.5 (38)cm

13 (14)"/33 (35.5)cm

CAPTIVATING CANTERBURY CAPELET

Starting with a stylish edging worked from the bottom up in seed stitch, this is a quick, easy knit. The unusual seed stitch cord tie is knit separately and sewn on to add dimension and beauty to the capelet. You'll want to make this in every beautiful Guanaco color.

FINISHED MEASUREMENTS

Approximately 16"/40.5cm high × 32"/81.5cm wide (before decreases)

MATERIALS

*4 3½oz/100g skeins (each approx 145yds/133m) of Aslan Trends Guanaco (60% alpaca, 40% merino wool) in #172 red
*Size 13 (9mm) knitting needles, OR SIZE NEEDED TO OBTAIN GAUGE
*Size 10½ (6.5mm) double-pointed needles (dpns)
*Tapestry needle

GAUGE

12 sts and 12 rows = 4"/10cm on size 13 (9mm) needles.
TAKE TIME TO CHECK GAUGE.

Note: Piece can be tied at side shoulder or center front.

Pattern Stitch

Seed Stitch (multiple of 2 sts + 1)
Row 1 K1, *p1, k1; rep from * across.
Rep Row 1 for Seed st patt always having a k st over a p st and a p st over a k st.

Shawl

With 2 strands of yarn held tog and size 13 needles, cast on 7 sts.
*Work 8 rows in Seed st. Cut yarn, leaving sts on needle; on same needle, cast on 7 sts; rep from * until there are 11 flaps (77 sts).

Connecting Row (RS) *K7, cast on 1 st; rep from *, end k7 (87 sts).
Continue in Seed st for 5".
Dec Row (RS) K1, p1, k1, p1, k1, *p1, k3tog; rep from * to la[st] 6 sts, p1, k1, p1, k1, p1, k1 (49 sts).
Continue in Seed st for 6"/15cm more.
Bind off in patt.

Seed Stitch Cord

With 2 strands of yarn held tog and dpns, cast on 5 sts.
Row 1 K1, *p1, k1; rep from * to end, do not turn; slide sts t[o] other end of needle.
Row 2 P1, *k1, p1; rep from * to end, do not turn; slide sts t[o] other end of needle.
Rep Rows 1 and 2 for 54"/137cm.
Leaving 11"/28cm of cord free, beg stitching the cord aroun[d] dec row. Let rem cord hang free.

Finishing

Weave in yarn ends.

ROMANTIC AUTUMN PULLOVER

ROMANTIC AUTUMN PULLOVER

Rich Del Cerro colors are abundant in the roses on this cinched-waist pullover. The full ribbed turtleneck and cuffs are in bold contrast to the patterned lace edge. Note the unusual knotting used on the cord ties.

SIZES: SMALL (MEDIUM)

FINISHED MEASUREMENTS
Bust: 40 (44)".101.5 (111.5)cm
Length: 32 (33)"/81.5 (84)cm

MATERIALS
*8 (10) 1¾oz/50g skeins (each approx 127yds/115m)
of AslanTrends Del Cerro (100% merino wool) in
#2129 café (MC)
*1 skein each in:
#3578 calabaza
#1364 yellow
#3315 fern
#4784 kiwi
#0009 sour apple
#0002 maize
*Sizes 7 (8)/4.5 (5)mm straight and circular 16"/40cm-long
needles, OR SIZE NEEDED TO OBTAIN GAUGE
*Size 5 (3.75mm) double-pointed needles (dpns)
*Stitch holders or waste yarn
*Straight pins
*Tapestry needle

GAUGES
18 sts and 22 rows = 4"/10cm in St st using size 7
(4.5mm) needles;
16 sts and 20 rows = 4"/10 cm in St st using size 8 (5mm)
needles. TAKE TIME TO CHECK GAUGE.

Pattern I
(multiple of 23 sts)
K 2 rows.
Row I (RS) *K8, k2tog, yo, k1, p1, k1, yo, ssk, k8; rep from *.
Row 2 *P7, p2tog tbl, p2, yo, k1, yo, p2, p2tog, p7; rep from *.
Row 3 *K6, k2tog, k1, yo, k2, p1, k2, yo, k1, ssk, k6, rep from *.
Row 4 *P5, p2tog tbl, p3, yo, p1, k1, p1, yo, p3, p2tog, p5;
rep from *.
Row 5 *K4, k2tog, k2, yo, k3, p1, k3, yo, k2, ssk, k4; rep from *.
Row 6 *P3, p2tog tbl, p4, yo, p2, k1, p2, yo, p4, k2tog, p3;
rep from *.
Row 7 *K2, k2tog, k3, yo, k4, p1, k4, yo, k3, ssk, k2; rep from *.
Row 8 *P1, p2tog tbl, p5, yo, p3, k1, p3, yo, p5, k2tog, p1;
rep from *.
Row 9 *K2tog, k4, yo, k5, p1, k5, yo, k4, ssk; rep from *.
Row 10 *P11, k1, p11; rep from *.
Row 11 *K11, p1, k11; rep from *.
Row 12 Rep row 10.
K 4 rows.

Back
With size 7 (8) straight needles and MC, cast on 92 sts + 2
selvage sts—94 sts.
Work in Patt I.
Change to St st and work until piece measures 17 (18)"/
43 (46)cm from beg, end with WS row.

Raglan Shaping
Bind off 5 sts at beg of next 2 rows—84 sts.

ec Row (RS) K2, ssk, k to last 3 sts, k2tog, k2.

II WS rows Purl.

ep last 2 rows 21 times more; 40 sts rem.

ace sts on holder.

ront

Vork same as Back, rep raglan dec row every other row 12

mes, 60 sts rem.

leck Shaping

(S) K2, ssk, k13, place sts on holder; bind off 26 sts, k13, k2tog, k2.

Vorking each side separate, at right neck edge bind off 1 st

very other row 4 times; AT THE SAME TIME, continue raglan

haping every other row 9 times more, 3 sts rem.

ace on holder.

everse for left neck shaping.

leeves

Vith size 7 (8) straight needles and MC, cast on 45 sts.

Vork in k1, p1 rib for 4"/10cm.

(S) K 1 row inc 1 st each side, then every 8th row 7 times

nore—59 sts. Continue until sleeve measures 17"/43cm from

eg, end with WS row.

aglan Shaping

ind off 5 sts at beg of next 2 rows.

Vork raglan shaping same as Back until 5 sts rem.

lace sts on holder.

inishing

ew Sleeves into Back and Fronts.

leck

Vith RS facing and circular needle size 7 (8), pick up and k

24 sts around neck edge including sts on holders. Join placing

narker at beg of round. Work in k1, p1 rib for 8"/20.2cm.

ind off loosely in rib.

mbroidery (see Techniques section, page 55)

Jsing duplicate st, follow chart for motifs and colors for Front,

Back and Sleeves. Use photos as guide for rose placement.

Sew sides and sleeve seams.

Weave in all ends.

Cord

With MC and double-pointed needles, CO 3 sts.

*K3 sts, slide to RH needle (do not turn work); rep from *

until 8 ft/2.44m long.

Slip 1, k2tog, psso. Tie off rem st.

Drawstring

Place a safety pin on one end of cord. Beg at center Front

weaving in-and-out every 2–3 sts at the waist back to center

Front. Make a knot at each end of cord. Note: ¼"/.5cm-wide

ribbon may also be used for drawstring.

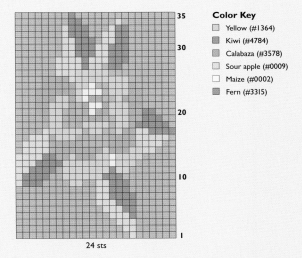

Color Key
- Yellow (#1364)
- Kiwi (#4784)
- Calabaza (#3578)
- Sour apple (#0009)
- Maize (#0002)
- Fern (#3315)

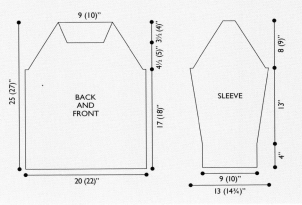

COZY CABLE COAT

This coat is made using Los Andes and Del Sur for fun, quick knitting. The contrasting colored cables, short sleeves and shawl color all work together to create casual elegance. And if that isn' enough, the Nicky Epstein Lillies front closures give the piece extra panache.

SIZES: SMALL/MEDIUM (LARGE/X-LARGE)

FINISHED MEASUREMENTS
Bust: 43 (47)"/109 (119.5)cm
Length: 28 (29)"/71 (73.5)cm

MATERIALS
*9 (10) 3½oz/100g skeins (each approx 87yds/80m) of Aslan Trends Los Andes (85% merino wool, 15% polyamide) in #1321 indigos (A)
*1(2) 3½oz/100g skeins (each approx 87yds/80m) of Aslan Trends Del Sur (100% merino wool) in #0014 azul (B)
*Size 13 (9mm) needles, OR SIZE TO OBTAIN GAUGE
*Cable needle
*Stitch markers
*Stitch holders
*Blunt tapestry needle
*Two Nicky Epstein #4044 Lillies clasps
(www.nickyepstein.com)

GAUGE
10 sts and 15 rows = 4"/10cm in St st on size 13 (9mm) needle. TAKE TIME TO CHECK GAUGE.

Note: Wind A and B on separate bobbins. When changing colors, pick up new color from under dropped color to prevent holes.

Cable Pattern (worked on 8 sts)
Foundation Row (RS) With B, k8.
Rows 1 and 3 (WS) K1, p6, k1.
Row 2 (RS) P1, k6, p1.
Row 4 P1, sl next 3 sts to cn and hold in front, k3, then k3 from cn, p1.
Rows 5–8 Rep Rows 1 and 2 twice more.
Rep Rows 1–8 for Cable Patt.

Back
With A, cast on 54 (58) sts.
Knit 3 rows.
Next row (WS) Purl.
**Work in St st for 4"/10cm, end with a WS row.
Est cable patt:
Foundation Row (RS) With A k5 (6), *join B and k 8, join ar other ball of A and k10 (11); rep from * once more, join B and k8, join A and k5 (6).
Row 1 (WS) With A p5 (6), *with B work Row 1 of Cable Patt on next 8 sts, with A p10 (11); rep from * once more, with B work Row 1 of Cable Patt on next 8 sts, with A p5 (6).
Row 2 (RS) With A k5 (6), *with B work Row 2 of Cable Patt on next 8 sts, with A k10 (11); rep from * once more, with B work Row 2 of Cable Patt on next 8 sts, with A k5 (6).
Row 3 (WS) With A p5 (6), *with B work Row 3 of cable patt on next 8 sts, with A p10 (11); rep from * once more, with B work Row 3 of Cable Patt on next 8 sts, with A p5 (6).
Row 4 (RS) With A k5 (6), *with B work Row 4 of Cable Patt on next 8 sts, with A k10 (11); rep from * once more, with B work Row 4 of Cable Patt on next 8 sts, with A and k5 (6).
Rows 5–8 Rep Rows 1 and 2 twice more. Work as est until Rows 1–8 of Cable Patt have been worked twice more.**

Rep from ** to ** once more. Continue in St st until piece measures 26"/66cm from beg, end with a WS row.

Shape raglan armhole

Bind off 4 sts at beg of next 2 rows—46 (50) sts.
Row 1 (RS) K1, ssk, k to last 3 sts, k2tog, k1.
Row 2 (WS) Purl.
Rep last 2 rows until 18 sts rem.
Bind off.

Right Front

With A, cast on 30 (32) sts.
Row 1 (RS) K1, p1 rib on first 6 sts, place marker (pm), k rem 24 (26) sts.
Row 2 (WS) P to marker, work last 6 sts in k1, p1 rib.
Row 3 K1, p1 rib on first 6 sts, k24 (26).
Row 4 P to marker, work last 6 sts in k1, p1 rib.
Rep last 2 rows until piece measures same as Back to beg of 2nd cable.
Est Cable Patt:
Foundation Row (RS) With A rib 6 and k8 (9), join B and k8, join another ball of A and k8 (9).
**Row 1 (WS) With A p8 (9), with B work Row 1 of Cable Patt on next 8 sts, with A p8 (9) and rib 6.
Row 2 (RS) With A rib 6 and k8 (9), with B work Row 2 of Cable Patt, with A k8 (9).
Rows 3–8 Work as est continuing until Row 8 of Cable Patt

is completed.**
Rep from ** to ** twice more.
Return to working 6 sts at front edge in rib and rem sts in St st with A only until piece measures approx 20"/51cm from beg, end with a WS row.

Shape collar and raglan armhole

Row 1 (RS) Rib 6, M1, sl marker, k rem sts.
Row 2 P to marker, rib 7.
Rep last 2 rows continuing collar incs 12 more working inc sts in rib—43 (45) sts; AT THE SAME TIME, when piece measures same as Back to armhole, shape raglan armhole same as Back. Place rem 25 sts on a holder for collar

Left Front

Work as for Right front, reversing shaping and pattern placement.

Sleeves

With A, cast on 40 (44) sts.
Knit 3 rows.
Next row (WS) Purl.
Work in St st until piece measures 8"/20.2 from beg, end with a WS row.

Shape raglan armhole

Bind off 4 sts at beg of next 2 rows—32 (36) sts.

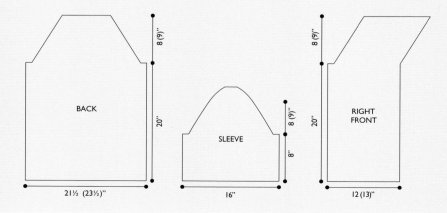

Row 1 (RS) K1, ssk, k to last 3 sts, k2tog, k1.

Row 2 Purl.

Rep last 2 rows until 4 sts rem. Bind off.

Finishing

Pin raglan seams.
Sew side and sleeve seams.

Collar: Place 25 sts from holder onto needle and continue in rib for 4½"/11.5cm. Bind off in rib. Work same on 25 sts on second holder. Join collar at center Back; sew to back neck.

Pockets (make 2)
With A, cast on 18 sts.
Work in St st for 2"/5cm, end with a WS row.

Est Cable Patt:

Foundation Row (RS) With A k5; join B and k8; join another ball of A and k5.

*Row 1 (WS) With A p5; with B work row 1 of Cable Patt on next 8 sts, with A p5.

Row 2 (RS) With A k5, with B work row 2 of Cable Patt on next 8 sts, with A k5.

Rows 3–8 Work as est, continuing until row 8 of Cable Patt is completed.**
Rep from ** to ** twice more.
With A, continue in St st only for 1"/2.4cm, end with a RS row.
Knit 1 row on WS.
Bind off.

Sew pockets to fronts as pictured. Sew closures to front following photo.

BEWITCHING HOODED SCARF

BEWITCHING HOODED SCARF

Classic counterpane blocks made with Artesanal and trimmed in fur make this a timeless fashion piece. Detailed point edging with corkscrews add to its striking look.

SIZE: ONE SIZE

FINISHED MEASUREMENTS
Width: 9½"
Length: 36" (not including tassels)

MATERIALS
*5 3½oz/100g skeins (each approx 218yds/200m) of Aslan Trends Artesanal (40% cotton, 30% alpaca, 30% polyamide)
*#0180 Raffia
*1 ½oz/15g skein (approx 3yds/2¾m) of Paula Lishman Fox Fur Yarn in cashmere (optional)
*Size 5 (3.75mm) needles,
OR SIZE NEEDED TO OBTAIN GAUGE

GAUGE
21 sts and 24 rows = 4"/10cm in St. st on size 5 (3.75mm) needles. TAKE TIME TO CHECK GAUGE.

ABBREVIATIONS
Inc 1K Knit into front and then back of st
Inc 1P Purl into back and then front of st

Bobble
Row 1 (RS) K into f, b, f, b of st—4 sts.
Row 2 K4.

Row 3 (K2tog) twice, sl 2nd st on RH needle over the 1st
Triangles: 4 triangles = 1 Block
Make 6 blocks and 2 single triangles
Cast on 1 st.
Row 1 RS: Inc 1K—2 sts.
Row 2 K1, Inc 1K—3 sts.
Row 3 K2, Inc 1K—4 sts.
Row 4 K3, Inc 1K—5 sts.
Rows 5–13 K to last st, Inc 1K—14 sts at end of row 13.
Row 14 P 13, Inc 1P—15 sts.
Row 15 K 14, Inc 1K—16 sts.
Row 16 P 15, Inc 1P—17 sts.
Row 17 (K2, p2) 4 times, Inc 1K—18 sts.
Row 18 P2 (k2, p2) 3 times, k2, p1, Inc 1K—19 sts.
Row 19 P1 (k2, p2) 4 times, k1, Inc 1K—20 sts.
Row 20 K1 (p2, k2) 4 times, p2, Inc 1K—21 sts.
Row 21 (P2, k2) 5 times, Inc 1P—22 sts.
Row 22 P 21, Inc 1P—23 sts.
Row 23 K 22, Inc 1K—24 sts.
Row 24 P 23, Inc 1P—25 sts.
Row 25 K 24, Inc 1K—26 sts.
Row 26 K 25, Inc 1K—27 sts.
Row 27 K 26, Inc 1K—28 sts.
Row 28 K 27, Inc 1K—29 sts.
Row 29 K 28, Inc 1K—30 sts.
Row 30 K 29, Inc 1K – 31 sts.
Row 31 K 30, Inc 1K—32 sts.
Row 32 K 31, Inc 1K—33 sts.

Row 33 K 32, Inc 1K—34 sts.
Row 34 K 33, Inc 1K—35 sts.
Row 35 K 2 (yo, k 2 tog) 16 times in 1K, 36 sts.
Row 36 K 35, Inc 1K—37 sts.
Row 37 K 36, Inc 1K—38 sts.
Row 38 P 37, Inc 1P—39 sts.
Row 39 K2 (bobble, k4) 7 times, bobble, Inc 1K—40 sts.
Row 40 P 39, Inc 1P—41 sts.
Row 41 K 40, Inc 1K—42 sts.
Row 42 K41, Inc 1K—43 sts.
Row 43 K2 (yo, k 2 tog) 20 times, Inc 1K—44 sts.
Row 44 K 43: Inc 1K—45 sts.
Row 45 K 44, Inc 1K—46 sts.
Row 46 P 45, Inc 1P—47 sts.
Row 47 K 46, Inc 1K—48 sts.
Bind off.

Finishing

Blocks (make 6)
Sew 4 triangles tog to make a block. Sew the 6 blocks tog in a strip. Sew a triangle at each end as in photo.

Hood: Sew back seam of center 2 blocks tog for hood. With corresponding thread, sew fur to scarf following photo.

Corkscrew tassels (make 6)
Cast 23 sts on loosely over 2 needles.
Row 1 (K1 f & b), k 1 in each st.
Row 2 Bind off all sts purlwise.
Use your fingers to twist and sqeeze each tassel into a corkscrew. Tie 3 tassels to each end point.

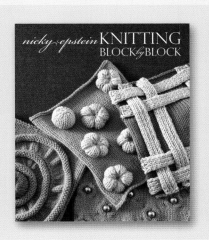

For more amazingly creative block designs see Nicky's

book **Nicky Epstein Knitting Block by Block**

(Potter Craft, November 2010)

HEAVENLY CARDIGAN SHAWL

HEAVENLY CARDIGAN SHAWL

Crochet and wear this amazing haute couture piece made with Invernal. The petite beaded flowers and front butterflied edges will make you the queen of your realm.

SIZE: ONE SIZE FITS MOST

FINISHED MEASUREMENTS
Bust: 44"/111.5cm
Length: 20"/51cm

MATERIALS
*6 3½oz/100g skeins (each approx 295yds/270m) of Aslan Trends Invernal (50% angora, 25% merino wool, 25% polyamide) in #59 sky
*Size G/6 (4mm) crochet hook,
OR SIZE NEEDED TO OBTAIN GAUGE
*97 Pearls beads

GAUGE
9 (dc, ch 1) = 4"/10cm with size G/6 (4mm) hook. TAKE TIME TO CHECK GAUGE.

Mesh Body (make 2)
Ch 212.
Row 1 Dc in 2nd ch from hook and in each ch across, ch 2, turn—210 dc. Note: Ch 2 counts as 1 dc and ch 1.
Row 2 *Dc in next dc, ch 1; rep from * end dc in 2nd ch of turning ch, ch2.
Rows 3–26 Rep row 2. After Row 26, DO NOT TURN.
Row 27 Cont across 26 rows (narrow end), ch 1, dc in next sp made by dc of Row 25, ch 1, dc in sp made by dc of Row 24. Cont to (ch 1, dc in next sp) to Row 1. Ch 2, turn.
Row 28 Skip 1st dc, dc in next dc, *ch 1, dc in next dc; rep from * across. Ch 2, turn.
Row 29 Dec 1 st each end as follows: Skip 1 dc, *dc in next dc, ch 1; rep from * to last 2 dc, 1 dc in next dc, leave 1 dc unworked. Ch 2, turn.
Rows 30–35 Rep Row 29 (4 dc rem). Ch 2, sl st to top of next dc. Fasten off.

Leaf (make 14)
Ch 18.
Sc in 5th ch from hook, (ch 3, sk 3, sc in next ch) 3 times, 3 sc in last ch, continue around to other side of ch, 4 sc in next sp, sc in next st, 4 hdc in next sp, hdc in next st, 4 dc in next sp, dc in next st, 4 tr in center opposite sp, tr in next sc, 4 dc in next sp, dc in next sc, 4 hdc in next sp, hdc in next sc, 4 sc in next sp, sl st in 1st sc to join, sl st all around leaf. Fasten off.

Flower Clusters
Strings of 6: make 1
Strings of 5: make 4
Strings of 4: make 6
Strings of 3: make 1
Strings of 2: make 8
String of 1: make 7
String of 17: make 1

First Flower
Ch 4.
In the 4th ch from hook work (2 dc cluster, ch 3, sl st)—first

etal made, in same space work *(ch 3, 2 dc cluster,
h 3, sl st)—next petal made; rep from * 2 more times
4 petals created).

or each additional flower in the string work as follows:
*Ch 9.
n 4th ch from hook work a (2 dc cluster, ch 3, sl st)—first
etal made, in same space work *(ch 3, 2 dc cluster, ch 3, sl
t)—next petal made; rep from * 2 more times.** Rep from
* to ** for each flower you would like to add to the string.

Butterfly (make 2)

Ch 24.

Rnd 1 Sc in 2nd ch from hook, sc in each of next 5 ch, hdc
n each of next 9 ch, dc in each of next 5 ch, sc in next ch,
dc in last ch. DO NOT TURN, cont along other side of
h, sc in next ch, dc in next 5 ch, hdc in each of next 9 ch,
c in each of next 5 ch, sl st in beg sc. DO NOT TURN,
ont around.

Rnd 2 Sl st in next 5 sts, *dc in next st, (ch 1, sk 1, 1 dc) 7
mes. Ch 2, turn.

Rnd 3 4 dc in next 2 ch-1 sps. Ch 3, turn.

Rnd 4 Sk 2 dc, sc in next dc, (ch 3, sk 2 dc, sc in next dc)
wice. Ch 3, turn.

Rnd 5 4 tr in 1st ch-3 sp, 5 dc in next ch-3 sp, 5 sc in last
h-3 sp. Ch 1, turn.

Rnd 6 Sc in each of next 4 sc, dc in each of next 5 dc, tr in
each of next 4 tr. Ch 3, turn.

Rnd 7 (Sk 2 tr, dc in next tr, ch 2) 3 times, sk 1 dc, dc in next
c, sk 1 st, sc in next sc, ch 2, sc in last st. Ch 1, turn.

Rnd 8 5 sc in 1st sp, 5 hdc in next sp, 5 dc in next sp, 5 tr in
next sp, 5 dtr in next sc. Ch 3, turn.

Rnd 9 Dtr in each of next 4 dtr, tr in each of next 5 tr, dc in
each of next 5 dc, hdc in each of next 5 hdc, sc in each of
next 4 sc. DO NOT TURN, cont working down wing toward body. Sl st in next st, ch 3, sk next sp, dc in next st, ch
, sk next sp, dc in next st, ch 2, sl st to top of next dc on
utterfly body (4th dc from butterfly head), sl st into next 4
ps. Ch 1, turn.

Rnd 10 3 sc in next sp, 2 dc in each of next 2 sps, sk next
sp on body, 2 dc in next sp, 4 tr in next sp. Ch 3, turn.

Rnd 11 Tr in each of next 4 tr, ch 2, sk 2 dc, dc in each of
next 4 dc, sc in next 2 sts. Ch 3, turn.

Rnd 12 Sk 2 sc, dc in next dc, ch 3, sk 2 dc, sp and 2 tr, dc in
next st, ch 3, sc in 3rd ch of beg ch 3. Ch 3, turn.

Rnd 13 5 tr in 1st sp, 5 dc in next sp, 5 sc in next sp, sl st
down wing. End off.

Antenna

With RS of butterfly facing, attach yarn to right side of top
of head, ch 12. Sl st in 2nd ch from hook and sl st back
down ch to butterfly head, sl st in next st on butterfly head,
ch 12, sl st in 2nd ch from hook and in each rem ch, sl st in
next st on butterfly head. End off.

Rep from Rnd 2 for other side of butterflies.

Finishing

Fold left and right sides in half, mark neck edge of each
side for shoulders. Unfold and place right sides of each
piece together and sew 9" down to make center back of
shawl. After the back of the shawl is sewn from neck edge
to center back, take the right side loose piece of the back
and line it up with the left side of the front edge piece,
then slip stitch them together. Rep for the left side back
loose piece and line it up with the right front edge.
Note: This also makes the armholes.

Attach butterflies, flowers, & leaves as follows

Butterflies; sew one to each side of bottom front edge.
Sew a pearl bead to end of each antennae.

Flowers & leaves; (use the beads to secure the centers of
each flower to the sweater). Thread a needle that fits
through the bead hole and tack down the 17-flower
string evenly around the neckline, placing a bead in each
flower center. For the back of the sweater, place a 6-
flower (cont. on page 52)

BEGUILING EMPIRE JACKET

BEGUILING EMPIRE JACKET

Always in style, this lightweight, easy to knit and wear piece is made with stockinette stitch using Artesanal. It has a colorful front-band stripping with a cord-flower corsage. A bow at the back wraps it all up.

SIZES: SMALL/MEDIUM (LARGE/X-LARGE)

FINISHED MEASUREMENTS
Bust: 43 (47)"/109 (119.5)cm
Length: 28½ (29½)"/72.5 (75)cm

MATERIALS
*4 (5) 3½oz/100g skeins (each approx 218yds/200m) of AslanTrends Artesanal (40% cotton, 30% alpaca, 30% polyamide) in #191 avocado (A)
*1 skein each in #4861 bright gold (B), #2979 terracotta (C) and #0135 eggplant (D)
*Size 9 (5.5mm) needles,
OR SIZE NEEDED TO OBTAIN GAUGE
*Size 8 (5mm) double-pointed needed (dpns)
*Stitch markers
*Stitch holders
*Blunt tapestry needle

GAUGE
16 sts and 24 rows = 4"/10cm in St st on size 9 (5.5mm) needles. TAKE TIME TO CHECK GAUGE.

Back
With A, cast on 120 (128) sts.
Work in Garter st (k every row) for ½"/1.2cm, end with a RS row.
Next Row (WS) Purl.
Work in St st until piece measures 14"/35.4cm from beg, end with a WS row.
Dec Row (RS) K20, k2tog across to last 20 sts, k20—80 (84) sts.
Continue in St st for 6", end with a WS row.

Shape armholes
Bind off 5 sts at beg of next 2 rows, then 2 sts at beg of next 2 rows. Dec 1 st each side every other row 4 times—58 (62) sts. Continue until armhole measures 8½ (9½)"/21.5 (24)cm. Bind off all sts.

Left Front
With A, cast on 60 (64) sts.
Work in Garter st (k every row) for ½"/1.2cm, end with a RS row.
Next Row (WS) Purl.
Work in St st until piece measures 14"/35.4cm from beg, end with a WS row.
Dec Row (RS) K2tog across row—30 (32) sts.
Continue in St st for 6"/15.2cm, end with a RS row.

Shape armhole
Shape armhole to correspond to Back—19 (21) sts.
Continue until armhole measures 8½ (9½)"/21.5 (24)cm. Bind off all sts.

Right Front
Work to correspond to Left Front, reversing shaping.

Sleeves

With A, cast on 56 (60) sts.
Work in Garter st for ½"/1.2cm, end with a RS row.
Next Row (WS) Purl.
Work in St st for 6"/15.2cm, end with a WS row.

Shape cap

Bind off 5 sts at beg of next 2 rows, 2 sts at beg of next 2 rows. Dec 1 st each edge every other row until 12 sts rem. Bind off 2 sts at beg of next 2 rows. Bind off rem 8 sts.

Finishing

Sew shoulder seams. Sew in Sleeves; sew sleeve and side seams.

Front Band

With A, cast on 40 sts.
Work in Garter st for ½"/1.2cm, end with a WS row.
Work in St st in following stripe pattern until band fits around front edges of jacket. End by working ½"/1.2cm in Garter st with A.
2 rows A, (2 rows C, 2 rows A) twice, 14 rows C;
(2 rows B, 2 rows C) 3 times, 14 rows B;
(2 rows D, 2 rows B) 3 times, 14 rows D;
(2 rows A, 2 rows D) 3 times, 14 rows A;
(2 rows C, 2 rows A) 3 times, 14 rows C;
(2 rows B, 2 rows C) 3 times, 14 rows B;
(2 rows D, 2 rows B) 3 times, 14 rows D.

(2 rows C, 2 rows D) 3 times, 14 rows C;
(2 rows B, 2 rows C) 3 times, 14 rows B;
(2 rows A, 2 rows B) 3 times, 14 rows A;
(2 rows D, 2 rows A) 3 times; 14 rows D;
(2 rows C, 2 rows D) twice, 4 rows C.
Bind off.

With RS of Front Band facing RS of jacket, sew band up Right Front, around Back Neck and down Left Front. Fold Front Band in half and sew to inside of jacket.

Back Bow

With B, cast on 12 sts.
Work in Garter st for ½"/1.2cm, end with a RS row.
Next Row (WS) Purl.
Work in St st until piece measures 5"/12.5cm.
Work in Garter st for ½"/1.2cm.
Bind off.

Bow Center Tie

With B, cast on 5 sts.
Work in Garter st for 1½"/3.7cm.
Bind off.

Wrap the 1½"/3.7cm center tie around the center of the Bow to gather; stitch in place. Sew Bow to Back Center above the dec gather row. **(cont. on page 52)**

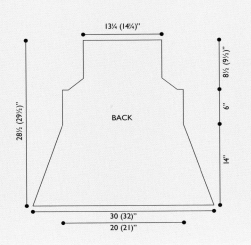

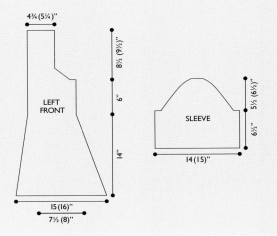

DELIGHTFUL BROCADE JACKET

DELIGHTFUL BROCADE JACKET

Using Invernal makes this cropped jacket a lovely, lightweight, go-anywhere fashion piece. It is box-shaped with deep ribs and ¾ sleeves, slightly gathered at the top with a full, folded rib cuff. The contrasting colorwork in short/long straight stitch and French knots creates beautiful embossed florals, giving the piece distinctive texture.

SIZES: SMALL/MEDIUM (LARGE/X-LARGE)

FINISHED MEASUREMENTS
Bust: 40 (44)"/101.5 (111.5)cm
Length: 18 (20)"/45.5 (51)cm

MATERIALS
*5 (6) 3½oz/100g skeins (each approx 295yds/270m) of AslanTrends Invernal (50% angora, 25% merino wool, 25% polyamide) in #46 wine (A)
*1 skein in #0041 fuchsia (B)
*Size 5 (3.75mm) needles,
OR SIZE NEEDED TO OBTAIN GAUGE
*Blunt tapestry needle
*One Nicky Epstein #4045 Fleur de Lis clasp (www.nickyepstein.com)

GAUGE
20 sts and 28 rows = 4"/10cm in St st. TAKE TIME TO CHECK GAUGE.

Back
With A, cast on 99 (111) sts.
Work in k3, p3 rib for 4½ (5)"/11.4 (12.5)cm from CO.
Beg on RS, work in St st until 10 (11)"/25.4 (27.8)cm, end with a WS row.

Shape armholes
Bind off 5 sts at beg of next 2 rows—89 (101) sts. Dec1

st each side every other row 6 times—77 (89) sts.
Work even until armhole measures 8 (9)"/20.2 (22.7)cm. Place sts on a spare needle.

Left Front
With A, cast on 51 (57) sts.
Work in k3, p3 rib for 4½ (5)"/11.4 (12.5)cm from CO.
Beg on RS, work in St st until 10 (11)"/25.4 (27.8)cm, end with a WS row.

Shape armhole
Shape armhole to correspond with back—40 (46) sts.
Continue until armhole measures 5 (6)"/12.5 (15.1)cm, end with RS row.

Shape neck
With WS facing, bind off 8 sts at neck edge once, 3 sts once, 2 sts once, then dec 1 st every other row 3 times—24 (30) sts.
Continue until armhole measures same as back.
Place sts on a spare needle.

Right Front
Work same as left front, reversing shaping.

Sleeves
With A, cast on 75 sts.
Work in k3, p3 rib for 6"/15.1cm.
Beg on RS, work in St st inc 1 st each side every 6th row 3

) times—81 (85) sts.
ontinue until piece measures 12 (13)"/30.5 (33)cm from
eginning or desired length, end with a WS row.

hape cap
nd off 5 sts at beg of next 2 rows. Dec 1 st each side
ery RS row 23 (25) times—25 sts rem.
S) K3tog 7 times, end k4tog.
VS) Purl 1 row.
nd off rem 8 sts.

inishing
in shoulder seams using Three-Needle Bind-Off (see
chniques section, page 52). Stitches may also be bound
f and sewn tog.

ront Band
/ith RS facing, pick up approx 90 (102) sts along left front
dge. Work in k3, p3 rib for 4"/10cm. Bind off in rib. Fold
ound-off edge of front band rib to inside cast-on edge
nd sew in place; sewing bottom rib together.
epeat for right front edge.

ew in sleeves; sew side and sleeve seams.

/ith B, embroider flowers using short and long straight
itches with French knot centers (see detail photos, right,
nd also page 56).

ollar
/ith RS facing and A, pick up 117 sts

around neck. Work in k3, p3 rib for 7"/17.8cm. Bind off in
rib. Fold bound-off edge of collar rib to inside and sew in
place; sewing a seam at each front edge of collar.

Sew on clasp following photo. Weave in yarn ends.

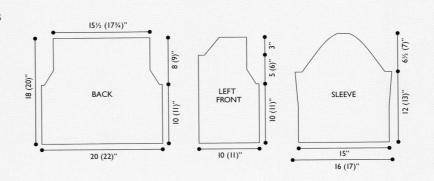

CHARMING LEAVES SHRUG/SCARF

CHARMING LEAVES SHRUG/SCARF

Made with Santa Fe, it's "too cute for words" with leaf cuffs and leaf cord tied at the back—irresistible! Wear it as a shrug or a scarf.

SIZES: SMALL/MEDIUM (LARGE/X-LARGE)

MATERIALS

*5 (6) 1¾oz/50g skeins (each approx 180yds/165m) of
AslanTrends Santa Fe (85% merino wool/15% polyamide)
in #1324 earth seasons
*Size 3 (3.25mm) and size 5 (3.75mm) needles for sm/med,
size 4 (3.5mm) and 6 (4mm) needles for lge/xl, OR SIZES
NEEDED TO OBTAIN GAUGE
*Size 4 (3.5mm) double-pointed needles (dpns)

GAUGES

24 sts and 32 rows = 4"/10cm on size 5 (3.75mm) needles;
22 sts and 28 rows = 4"/10cm on size 6 (4mm) needles.
TAKE TIME TO CHECK GAUGE.

Embossed leaf stitch

(multiple of 7 sts plus 6)
Row 1 (RS) P6, *yo, k1, yo, p6; rep from * to end.
Rows 2 and 14 *K6,p3; rep from *, end k6.
Row 3 P6, *k1, yo, k1, yo, k1, p6; rep from * to end.
Rows 4 and 12 *K6, p5; rep from *, end k6.
Row 5 P6, *k2, yo, k1, yo, k2, p6; rep from * to end.
Rows 6 and 10 *K6, p7; rep from *, end k6.
Row 7 P6, *k3, yo, k1, yo, k3, p6; rep from * to end.
Row 8 *K6, p9; rep from *, end k6.
Row 9 P6, *skp, k5, k 2 tog, p6; rep from * to end.
Row 11 P6, *skp, k3, k 2 tog, p6; rep from * to end.
Row 13 P6, *skp, k1, k 2 tog, p6; rep from * to end.
Row 15 P6, *sk2p, p6; rep from * to end.
Row 16 K.

Sleeves (make 2)
Cast on 62 sts.
Rows 1–3 K.

Rows 4–19 Work Rows 1–16 of Embossed Leaf Pattern
Row 20 (RS) P.
Row 21 K.
Row 22 K.
Rows 23–66 Rep Rows 1–22 two more times.
Rows 67 and 68 K.
Row 69 K, increase 0 (10) sts evenly across—62 (72) sts
Continue in reverse St st until piece measures 29 (31)"/
73.5 (78.5)cm or desired length. Leave sts on spare needle.

Finishing
Back seam: Placing right sides tog, needles pointing in the
same direction, with 3rd needle, *k 1 st from front needle
tog with 1 st from back needle and rep from * once; bind
off first st. Cont in this way until all sts are bound off. Sew
sleeve seams 17(19)"/43 (48)cm up from cast on edges. Let
edging roll naturally.
Cord Leaf Tie
I cord (see Techniques section, page 55)
With size 4 (3.5mm) dpns, cast on 5 sts. K 5, *do not turn work.
Slide sts to beg of dpn and k5; rep from * for I-cord until piece
measures 35"/89cm. Working back and forth, continue with leaf.

Leaf
Row 1 (RS) K2, yo, k1, yo, k2.
Row 2 and all WS rows Purl.
Row 3 K3, yo, k1, yo, k3.
Row 5 K4, yo, k1, yo, k4 - 11 sts.
Row 7 Ssk, k7, k 2 tog.
Row 9 Ssk, k5, k 2 tog.
Row 11 Ssk, k3, k 2 tog.
Row 13 Ssk, k1, k 2 tog.
Row 15 Sk2p.
Fasten off.
Pick up 5 sts from cast on edge and repeat leaf. (cont. on page 52)

ALLURING DIAMOND COAT

Here a combination of a classic diamond pattern and an original cable edging shape this hooded coat made to flatter any and all sizes. Note the creatively designed pockets. When you knit this with Guanaco, you are sure to be beautifully warm and cozy.

SIZES: SMALL (MEDIUM, LARGE)

FINISHED MEASUREMENTS
Bust: 42 (46, 50)"
Length: 31 (32, 33)"

MATERIALS
* 12 (13, 14) 3½oz/100g skeins (each approx 145yds/133m) of AslanTrends Guanaco (60% alpaca, 40% merino wool) in #51 rust
*Size 9 (5.5mm) and 10 (6mm) straight needle and SIZE 9 circular 47"/120cm-long needles, OR SIZE NEEDED TO OBTAIN GAUGE
*Cable needle
*Stitch markers
*Tapestry needle
*Seven Nicky Epstein buttons, #92722 "Dancing Sheep," (www.nickyepstein.com)

GAUGE
16 sts and 24 rows = 4"/10cm in overall patts. TAKE TIME TO CHECK GAUGE.

ABBREVIATIONS
2/2 LC Sl next 2 sts onto cable needle (cn) and hold at front of work, k next 2 sts from left-hand needle, then k sts from cable needle.

2/2 RC Sl next 2 sts onto cn and hold at back of work, k next 2 sts from left-hand needle, then k sts from cn.

2/2 LPC Sl next 2 sts onto cn and hold at front of work, p next 2 sts from left-hand needle, then k sts from cn.

2/2 RPC Sl next 2 sts onto cn and hold at back of work, k next 2 sts from left-hand needle, then p sts from cn.

Pattern Stitches
Pattern I a
(multiple of 4 sts)
Row 1 *K2, p2; rep from *.
Rep Row 1 for Patt I a.

Pattern I b
(multiple 4 sts + 2 sts)
Row 1 K2, *p2, k2; rep from *.
Row 2 P2, *k2, p2; rep from *.
Rep Rows 1–2 for Patt I b.

Pattern II
(multiple of 6 sts + 2)
Row 1 (WS) K3, p4, *k2, p4; rep from * to last st, k1.
Row 2 (RS) P1, 2/2 LC, *p2, 2/2 LC; rep from * to last 3 sts, p3.
Row 3 Rep Row 1
Row 4 P3, *k2, 2/2 RPC; rep form * to last 5 sts, k4, p1.
Row 5 K1, p4, *k2, p4; rep from * to last 3 sts, k3.
Row 6 P3, 2/2 RC, *p2, 2/2 RC; rep from * to last st, p1.
Row 7 Rep row 5.
Row 8 P1, k4, *2/2 RPC, k2; rep from * to last 3 sts, p3.
Rep these 8 rows for Patt II.

Pattern III

(multiple of 8 sts + 1)

Row 1 (WS) P3, *k1, p1, k1, p5; rep from *, end last rep p3

Row 2 (RS) K4, *p1, k7; rep form * to last 5 sts, p1, k4.

Row 3 P3, *k1, p1, k1, p5; rep from *, end last rep p3.

Row 4 K2, *p1, k3; rep from *, end last rep k2.

Row 5 P1, *k1, p5, k1, p1; rep from *.

Row 6 *P1, k7; rep from * to last st, p1.

Row 7 Rep row 4.

Row 8 Rep row 3.

Rep rows 1–8 for Patt III.

Back

With larger needles, cast on 116 (128, 140) sts.
Work patt I for 1¼"/3cm, ending with a RS row.
Beg on WS, work Patt II for 2 reps (3½"/8.7cm), end on RS with Patt Row 1 and dec 18 (24, 30) sts across row (do not dec in center 32 [38, 44] sts in order to maintain pattern integrity)—98 (104, 110) sts.
Est patt (WS) Work patt III on 33 sts, Patt II on next 32 (38, 44) sts, Patt III on rem 33 sts.
Continue in est patts until piece measures 16"/41cm from beg, ending with a RS row.
(WS) Work Patt III on 15 sts, Patt II on next 68 (74, 80) sts, Patt III on rem 15 sts.
Continue in est patts for 15 more rows, ending with a RS row.
Est patt (WS) Work Patt III on 33 sts, Patt II on next 32 (38, 44) sts, Patt III on rem 33 sts.
Continue in est patts until piece measures 23"/58.4cm from beg, ending with a WS row.

Shape armholes

Maintaining patts, bind off 5 sts at beg of next 2 rows—88 (94, 100) sts. Dec 1 st each side every other row 5 times—78 (84, 90) sts. Work even until armhole measures 8 (9, 10)"/20.7 (22.7, 25.4)cm. Bind off.

Left Front

With larger needles, cast on 56 (62, 68) sts.
Work Patt I for 1¼"/3cm, ending with a RS row.
Beg on WS, work Patt II for 2 reps (3½"/8.7cm), end on RS with Patt Row 1 and dec 15 (13, 11) sts evenly across row—41 (49, 57) sts.
Beg on WS, work Patt III until same length as back, end with a WS row.

Shape armhole

Shape armhole to correspond with back—31 (39, 47) sts.
Continue until armhole measures 7"/17.8cm, end with RS row.

Shape neck

Bind off 8 (9, 10) sts at neck edge once, then 2 sts every other row 1 (2, 3) time(s), 1 st every other row 1 (2, 3) times—20 (24, 28) sts.
Continue until armhole measures same as back.
Bind off rem sts.

Right Front

Work same as left front, reversing shaping.
Sew shoulder seams.

Sleeves

With smaller needles, cast on 56 (62, 68) sts.
Work st st for 1¼"/3cm. End WS.
Change to large needles.
(RS) P 1 row inc 1 (3, 5) st(s) evenly across—57 (65, 73) sts.
Beg on WS, work Patt III inc 1 st each side every 10th row 3 times, adjusting patt at edge as you inc—63 (71, 79) sts.
Continue until piece measures 18"/45.7cm (or desired length from beg.

Shape cap

Maintaining patt, bind off 4 sts at beg of next 2 rows. Dec 1 st each side every RS row 20 (24, 28) times—15 sts rem.
Bind off 2 sts at beg of next 4 rows. Bind off 7 rem sts.

Pockets (make 2)
Cast on 25 sts with larger needles.
Work Patt III for 5"/12.5cm, end with Patt Row 1.
(RS) K inc 13 sts evenly across row—38 sts.
Work Patt II for 2 reps, ending with a RS row.
(WS) P5, bind off 15 sts in p, p5.
(RS) *(K1, inc 1 st in next st) twice, k1 (7 sts)*; cast on 24
sts using Knitted Cast On from back of work, rep from *
to *—38 sts.
Beg on WS, continue in Patt II for 2 reps (3½"/8.7cm).
Bind off.

Hood
With RS facing and larger needles, pick up 73 (81, 89) sts
around neck.
Work Patt III for 10 (10 ½, 11)". Bind off.

RS tog, fold bound-off edge together and sew top seam.

Front Band
With RS facing and smaller circular needle, staring at lower
right front edge, pick up approx 112 (114, 116) sts to neck
shaping, 80 (84, 88) sts around hood, 112 (114, 116) sts
down left front—304 (312, 324) sts. Work Patt I for
1"/2.4cm; AT THE SAME TIME, work seven 2-st buttonholes evenly spaced on right front on 3rd and 4th row of
Patt I.
Buttonhole row (RS) Rib 4 (5, 6), bind off 2 sts, *rib 15,
bind off 2 sts; rep from * 6 times, end rib to end.
(WS) Rib and cast on 2 sts over each set of bound-off sts.
Bind off after 1"/2.4cm rib has been completed.

FInishing
Sew pockets to fronts (see photo)
Sew in sleeves, sew side and sleeve seams. Sew on buttons
to correspond with buttonholes.

Back Pleat
With RS of Back facing, place marker on hood seam at
center of patt II. Fold the edges of patt II panel to this
marker, forming a box pleat in Hood and Back. Sew pleat
in place along hood seam.

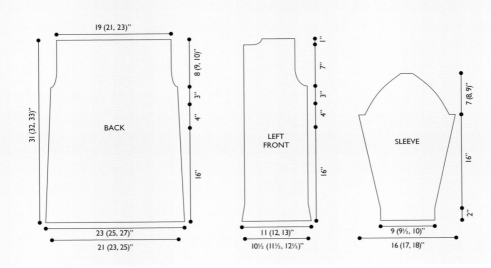

FASCINATING BELLE EPOQUE SHRUG

The "keys" to knitting success are beautiful yarns and a great design that's easy and quick to knit. Del Sur is a perfect yarn to make this piece for yourself or as a gift for loved ones.

SIZE: ONE SIZE

MATERIALS

*2 3½oz/100g skeins (each approx 87yds/80m) of AslanTrends Del Sur (100% merino wool) in #43 ash
*Size 13 (9mm) needles, OR SIZE NEEDED TO OBTAIN GAUGE

GAUGE

8 sts and 16 rows = 4"/10cm on size 13 (9mm) needles in St st. TAKE TIME TO CHECK GAUGE.

ABBREVIATIONS

2/3 LPC Sl 2 to cn and hold in front, p3, k2 from cn.
2/3 RPC Sl 3 to cn and hold in back, k2, p3 from cn.
3/3 LC Sl 3 sts to cn and hold in front, k3, k3 from cn.

Bell Cable Rib (multiple of 14 sts plus 2)
Rows 1, 3, 5, 7 and 9 (RS) *P2, k2, [p3, k2] twice; rep from *, end p2.
Row 2 and all WS Rows K the knit sts and p the purl sts.
Row 11 *P2, 2/3 LPC, k2, 2/3 RPC; rep from *, end p2.
Rows 13, 15 and 17 P5, *k6, p8; rep from *, end last rep p5.
Row 19 P5, *3/3 LC, p8; rep from *, end last rep p5.

Neckpiece

Starting at top, cast on 86 sts.
Rows 1–20 Work rows 1–10 of Bell Cable Rib Pattern twice.
Rows 21–29 Work rows 11–19 of Bell Cable Rib Pattern.
Rows 30–45 Work rows 16–19 of Bell Cable Rib Pattern

4 more times.
Row 46 Rep Pattern Row 2.
Bind off in pattern.

Finishing:

RS facing, pick up 43 sts along right side of piece.
Row 1 (WS) P1, * k1, p1; rep from *to end.
Row 2 K1, *p1, k1; rep from * to end.
Rep Rows 1 and 2 for 2"/5cm. Bind off in rib.

Left side:

Work same as for right side.

Note: Nicky Epstein Key Shawl Pin (www.nickyepstein.com)

BEDAZZLING WEDDING RING BODICE

BEDAZZLING WEDDING RING BODICE

This handmade beauty can be worn by the bride with a satin skirt for the wedding and then, after the wedding, as a top with jeans. AslanTrends Class is the perfect yarn to make this piece. An easy crochet-ring-stitch repeat (appropriate for weddings) is enhanced with sewn-on Swarovski Crystals. It really sparkles, and the open back is laced with tulle. Cord and ribbons or fabric can also be used.

FINISHED MEASUREMENTS
Bust: approx 21" (across bust and under arms)
Length: approx 22" from center of neck to bottom edge

MATERIALS
*5 3½oz/100g skeins (each approx 240yds/220m) of AslanTrends Class (55% cotton, 45% viscose) in #4019 straw
*Size E/4 (3.5mm) crochet hook,
OR SIZE TO OBTAIN GAUGE
*108 (8mm) Crystal Passions/Crystallized Swarovski Elements Beads
*57"/145cm crocheted I-cord, ribbon, or 3yds/2.74m of netting cut into 25"/61cm width
*Tapestry needle
*Small amount of fiberfill

GAUGE
1 ring (ch 10 circle + 24 dc) = 1.5"/3cm

Ring pattern
Ch 10, sl st to 1st ch to make a circle, ch 3 (counts as 1 dc), work total of 20 dc in circle, *ch 10, sl st to 1st ch to make 2nd circle, ch 3 (counts as 1 dc), work 12 dc in circle (this makes ½ a circle), repeat from * for length of circles needed, in last circle made work 24 dc in circle, continue down the other side to complete the other half of each circle already made as follows: ** work 1 sc in sl st between two circles, ch 3 (counts as 1 dc), work 12 dc in next circle, repeat from ** to last circle, work 1 sc in sl st between last two circles, ch 3, work 3 dc in last circle, end with sl st to 3rd st of beg. ch3, end off.

Motif patterns (make 4)
First Motif (make 2)
Work the above Ring Pattern for 12 rings, do not end off, do not turn, work (1 dc, 1 ch, 1 dc), in each of the next 17 dc, 1 dc in next dc, turn.
Rnd 2 Ch 3 (counts as 1 dc), work 3 dc cl: leaving last lp of each st on hook, work all 3 dc in same ch 1 lp, yo and draw thru all 4 lps on hook, ch 3, in each ch-1 loop around (17 clusters), turn.
Rnd 3 Sl st to top of 1st 3-dc-cl, ch 3, sl st in ch-3 sp, *ch 1 sl st in next ch-3 sp, ch 3, sl st in same ch-3 sp, rep from * to last ch-3 cl, sl st in top of last cl, end off.

Second Motif (make 2)
Work same as First Motif on 4 rings instead of 12 rings.

Button
Ch 2, work 6 sc in 2nd ch from hook, cont to sc in each sc in back loops only once more, insert sm amt of fiberfill, sc in each sc around, sc in next sc, sk next sc until one st is left on hook, sl st button closed.

I-cord
Ch 2, 5 sc in 2nd ch from hook, work 1 sc in back loops only of ea sc around for 57"/145cm.

To Make Bodice

Crochet the following lengths of rings:

-ring length—make 2.

-ring length—make 2 (ring pattern with motif pattern with crystals sewn in each motif).

-ring length—make 2.

-ring length—make 2.

-ring length—make 3 (with crystals sewn in each ring center of one).

10-ring length—make 1 (with crystals sewn in each of 9 ring centers; leave last ring to button).

2-ring length—make 2 (ring pattern with motif pattern with 8 crystals in each motif).

3-ring length—make 2 (with crystals sewn in only one 13 ring length centers).

*14-ring length—make 3 (sew crystals in 7 rings in two 14 ring length centers).

6-ring length—make 3 (sew crystals in 2 of the 16 ring lengths).

Do not end off after last loop is made, ch 6, make ball (for button) instructions above.

** 2 of the 14 ring lengths go around each arm to make the front armholes and back shoulder straps of bodice—only the back 7 rings have crystals sewn in.

To Assemble

Use the diagram to lay out the ring lengths with wrong sides up. Start with the 10-ring neck length and 8-ring neck length, sew them together by placing the tapestry needle threaded with yarn through corresponding crocheted stitches on each piece and whip stitching them loosely together over 5 or 6 stitches. Next attach the center front 13-ring length to center neck edge, next sew 1 of the 14 ring lengths (with the crystals toward the back) together to make a circle for the right armhole and attach to neck edge. Repeat for the left side. Continue attaching corresponding ring lengths to the left and right sides of the center front length, making sure to place the crystals where indicated on the diagram.

Back Swag

Sew a 13-, 14-, and 16-ring length together as shown on diagram, attach to right and left sides of bodice, being careful to leave the 3 back rings free for lacing the I-cord, netting or ribbon.

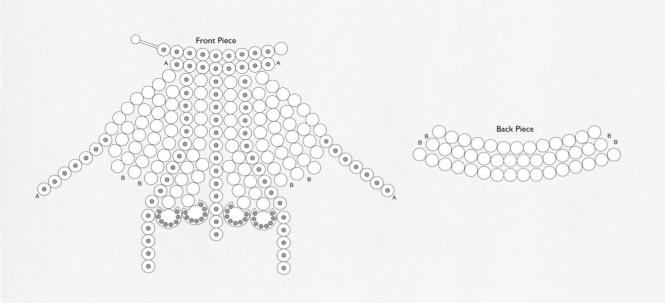

47

MAGICAL TWO-WAY CAPELET

MAGICAL TWO-WAY CAPELET

Using Pima Clasico cotton, four lovely blocks are sewn together in a unique method to create a double showstopper that can be worn two ways. (For more amazing block designs see Nicky Epstein's book *Knitting Block by Block*, published in November 2010 by Potter Craft.)

SIZES: SMALL/MEDIUM (LARGE)

MATERIALS
*5 1¾oz/50g skeins (each approx 111yds/101.5m) of Aslan-Trends Pima Clasico (100% pima cotton) in #0054 dahlia
*Size 7 (4.5mm) double-pointed needles (dpns), set of 5, OR SIZE NEEDED TO OBTAIN GAUGE
*Size 6 (4mm) dpns

GAUGE
20 sts and 26 rows = 4"/10cm in St st on size 7 (4.5mm) dpns. TAKE TIME TO CHECK GAUGE.

Note: Each line of instructions is repeated once on each needle.

Cast on 8 sts (2 sts each on 4 size 7 (4.5mm) dpns).
K 1 rnd.
Rnd 1 [Yo, k1] twice—4 sts.
Rnd 2 and all even rnds through Rnd 40 Knit.
Rnd 3 Yo, k1, yo, ssk, yo, k1.
Rnd 5 Yo, k 2 tog, yo, k1, yo, ssk, yo, k1.
Rnd 7 Yo, k 2, yo, p 3 tog, yo, k2, yo, k1.
Rnd 9 Yo, k1, k 2 tog, yo , k3, yo, ssk, k1, yo, k1.
Rnd 11 Yo, k3, yo, k1, p 3 tog, k1, yo, k3, yo, k 1—14 sts.
Rnd 13 Yo, k2, k 2 tog, yo, k5, yo, ssk, k2, yo, k1.
Rnd 15 Yo, k4, yo, k2, p 3 tog, k2, yo, k4, yo, k1.
Rnd 17 Yo, k3, k 2 tog, yo, k7, yo, ssk, k3, yo, k1.

Rnd 19 Yo, k5, yo, k3, p3 tog, k3, yo, k5, yo, k1.
Rnd 21 Yo, k4, k 2 tog, yo, k9, yo, ssk, k4, yo, k1—24 sts.
Rnd 23 Yo, k6, yo, k4, p 3 tog, k4, yo, k6, yo, k1.
Rnd 25 Yo, k5, k 2 tog, yo, k11, yo, ssk, k5, yo, k1.
Rnd 27 Yo, k7, yo, k5, p 3 tog, k5, yo, k7, yo, k1.
Rnd 29 Yo, k6, k2 tog, yo, k1, yo, ssk, k7, k 2 tog, yo, k1, yo, ssk, k6, yo, k1.
Rnd 31 Yo, k6, k 2 tog, yo, k3, yo, ssk, k5, k 2 tog, yo, k3, yo, ssk, k6, yo, k1—34 sts.
Rnd 33 [Yo, k1, yo, ssk, k3, k 2 tog, yo, k1, yo, sk2p] twice, yo k1, yo, ssk, k3, k 2 tog, yo, k1, yo, k1.
Rnd 35 Yo, k3, yo, [ssk, k1, k 2 tog, yo, k3, yo, ssk, k2, yo] twice, ssk, k1, k 2 tog, yo, k3, yo, k1.
Rnd 37 [Yo, k1, yo, sk2p] 9 times [yo, k1] twice.
Rnd 39 Yo, k3 [yo, ssk, k2] 9 times, yo, k1.
Rnd 41 [Yo, k1, yo, sk2p] 10 times, [yo, k1] twice—44 sts.
Bind off knitwise.
Make 4 blocks.
Sew blocks together following diagram.

Cord edging:
Cast on 5 sts. *K 5 sts. Do not turn work, slide 5 sts to right end of dpn, rep from * until cord is approximately 42"/106.5cm. Length fits around bottom edge with a tie at right corner. Rep cord for neck, approximately 20"/50.7cm. Measure cord 3½"/9cm up. Starting at a seam, sew rem cord around neck edge, leaving 3½"/9cm of cord rem at other end. Tie in knot. Repeat for bottom edge.

Flowers (make 4)

Make slip knot, *cast on 8 sts, bind off 8 sts. Slip remaining to left needle. Rep from * 8 times more. Run threaded eedle through bottom slip sts, pull tightly and secure. Sew ower to center of each block.

Note: Fabric glue can be used to tack flower in place.

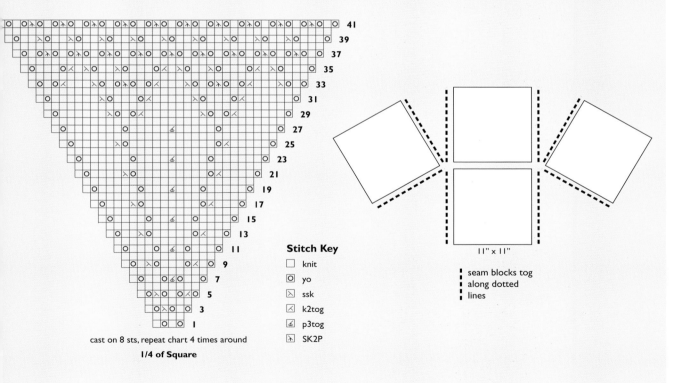

cast on 8 sts, repeat chart 4 times around

1/4 of Square

Stitch Key

☐	knit
O	yo
↘	ssk
↙	k2tog
↙	p3tog
↗	SK2P

11" x 11"

seam blocks tog
along dotted
lines

Continued...

BEGUILING EMPIRE JACKET **Continued from page 29**

Note: Bow can be made in any color you prefer.

Flowers (make 3)

With dpns, cast on 3 sts, work I-cord for approx 27"/68.5cm. Fold accordion-style until you have 8 petals (each petal should be approx 1½"/3.7cm). Run thread through inner points of petals, pull tightly and secure. Leave remaining cord hanging. Make a knot at the end of the cord. To make flower center, work I-cord 3"/7.5cm long; tie in knot. Repeat for other two flowers, varying size of petals. Sew flowers to lapel in desired arrangement. Place knotted cord in center of each flower, pull cast-on edge and bind-off edge through back and tie in place.

CHARMING LEAVES SHRUG/SCARF **Continued from page 37**

Leaf back (make 2)

Cast on 5 sts and work rows 1–15 of leaf.

With WS tog, sew leaf back to leaf on each cord end. Fold leaf cord in half and loop around center back of piece. Tie using photos as guide. Tack cord to center back seam.

HEAVENLY BUTTERFLY CARDIGAN SHAWL **Continued from page 25**

string evenly spaced below the 17-flower string, cont in this manner with the 3-, 2- and 1-flower strings. Sew down a leaf on each side of this back cluster of flowers.

Front placement: on right front neck edge, secure a 4-flower string alongside the 17-flower string, next secure a 2-flower string alongside the 4-flower string, end with 1 flower below the 2-flower string, working down the front edge, sew down a cluster of 3 leaves approx. 2" below the 17-flower string. End with one flower sewn in the center of the leaf cluster (see photo).

Below the cluster of leaves, secure a 5-flower string along the front edge; working toward the butterfly, attach a 5-, 4-, 2- then 1-flower string cluster. attach a leaf along front edge between flower cluster and butterfly wing. Work placement of flowers and leaves on left front to correspond with right front.

Sleeves: secure a 5-flower cluster to bottom of each sleeve and working toward the shoulders and front of sweater, attach a 4-, 2- and 1-flower string and 2 leaves toward the back of the sweater. Attach a 2-flower string alongside of leaf toward back.

Refer to photo for flower placement.

Details

CORD CLOSURE
Page 4

ROSE
Page 10

NICKY'S "LILLIES" CLASPS
Page 14

CORKSCREWS
Page 18

CORD FLOWERS
Page 26

BOW
Page 26

EMBROIDERED FLOWERS
Page 30

CORD LEAFTIE
Page 34

DIAMOND CABLE DETAIL
Page 38

FLOWER APPLIQUE
Page 48

"BUTTERFLY" MOTIF
Page 22

CROCHET BUTTON CLOSURE
Page 44

Abbreviations

KNITTING ABBREVIATIONS

approx	approximately	**M1**	make one (see glossary)	**S2KP**	slip 2 stitches together, knit 1, pass 2 slip stitches over knit 1
beg	begin(ning)	**M1 p-st**	make 1 purl stitch (see glossary)	**sl**	slip
CC	contrasting color	**oz**	ounce(s)	**sl st**	slip stitch (see glossary)
ch	chain	**p**	purl	**ssk**	slip, slip, knit (see glossary)
cm	centimeter(s)	**pat(s)**	pattern(s)	**sssk**	slip, slip, slip, knit (see glossary)
cn	cable needle	**pm**	place marker (see glossary)	**st(s)**	stitch(es)
cont	continu(e)(ing)	**psso**	pass slip stitch(es) over	**St st**	stockinette stitch
dec	decreas(e)(ing)	**p2tog**	purl two stitches together—one stitch has been decreased	**tbl**	through back loop(s)
dpn	double-pointed needle(s)			**tog**	together
foll	follow(s)(ing)			**WS**	wrong side(s)
g	gram(s)	**rem**	remain(s)(ing)	**wyib**	with yarn in back
inc	increas(e)(ing)	**rep**	repeat	**wyif**	with yarn in front
k	knit	**RH**	right-hand	**yd**	yard(s)
kfb	knit into the front and back of a stitch—one stitch has been increased	**RS**	right side(s)	**yo**	yarn over needle (U.K.: see glossary)
		rnd(s)	round(s)		
k2tog	knit 2 stitches together—one stitch has been decreased	**SKP**	slip 1, knit 1, pass slip stitch over—one stitch has been decreased	*****	repeat directions following * as many times as indicated
LH	left-hand			**[ ]**	repeat directions inside brackets as many times as indicated
lp(s)	loop(s)	**SK2P**	slip 1, knit 2 together, pass slip stitch over the knit 2 together—two stitches have been decreased		
m	meter(s)				
mm	millimeter(s)				
MC	main color				

CROCHET ABBREVIATIONS

BP	back post	**dc2tog**	double crochet 2 stitches together	**lp(s)**	loop(s)
BPdc	back post double crochet			**sc**	single crochet
BPsc	back post single crochet	**dtr**	double treble	**sc2tog**	single crochet 2 sts together
BPtr	back post treble crochet	**FP**	front post	**sk**	skip(ped)
ch	chain(s)	**FPdc**	front post double crochet	**sl st**	slip stitch
ch-	refers to chain or space previously made (i.e., ch-1 space)	**FPsc**	front post single crochet	**sp(s)**	space(s)
		FPtr	front post treble crochet	**t-ch**	turning chain
ch-sp	chain space previously made	**grp(s)**	group(s)	**tr**	treble
dc	double crochet	**hdc**	half double crochet	**trtr**	triple treble

Techniques

3-NEEDLE BIND-OFF

This bind-off is used to join two edges that have the same number of stitches, such as shoulder edges, which have been placed on holders.

1. With the right side of the two pieces facing each other, and the needles parallel, insert a third needle knitwise into the first stitch of each needle. Wrap the yarn around the needle as if to knit.

2. Knit these two stitches together and slip them off the needles. *Knit the next two stitches together in the same way as shown.

3. Slip the first stitch on the third needle over the second stitch and off the needle. Repeat from the * in step 2 across the row until all the stitches are bound off.

DUPLICATE STITCH

Duplicate stitch covers a knit stitch. Bring the needle up below the stitch to be worked. Insert the needle under both loops one row above and pull it through. Insert it back into the stitch below and through the center of the next stitch in one motion, as shown.

I-CORD

Using 2 double-pointed needles, cast on 3 to 5 stitches. *Knit one row on RS. Without turning the work, slip the stitches to right end of needle to work the next row on the RS. Repeat from * until desired length. Bind off.

Glossary

bind off Used to finish an edge or segment. Lift the first stitch over the second, the second over the third, etc. (U.K.: cast off)

bind off in ribbing Work in ribbing as you bind off. (Knit the knit stitches, purl the purl stitches.) (U.K.: cast off in ribbing)

3-needle bind-off With the right side of the two pieces facing and the needles parallel, insert a third needle into the first stitch on each needle and knit them together. Knit the next two stitches the same way. Slip the first stitch on the third needle over the second stitch and off the needle. Repeat for three-needle bind-off.

cast on Placing a foundation row of stitches upon the needle in order to begin knitting.

decrease Reduce the stitches in a row (that is, knit 2 together).

increase Add stitches in a row (that is, knit in front and back of stitch).

knitwise Insert the needle into the stitch as if you were going to knit it.

make one With the needle tip, lift the strand between the last stitch knit and the next stitch on the left-hand needle and knit into back of it. One knit stitch has been added.

make one p-st With the needle tip, lift the strand between the last stitch worked and the next stitch on the left-hand needle and purl it. One purl stitch has been added.

no stitch On some charts, "no stitch" is indicated with shaded spaces where stitches have been decreased or not yet made. In such cases, work the stitches of the chart, skipping over the "no stitch" spaces.

pick up and knit (purl) Knit (or purl) into the loops along an edge.

place markers Place or attach a loop of contrast yarn or purchased stitch marker as indicated.

purlwise Insert the needle into the stitch as if you were going to purl it.

selvage stitch Edge stitch that helps make seaming easier.

slip, slip, knit Slip next two stitches knitwise, one at a time, to right-hand needle. Insert tip of left-hand needle into fronts of these stitches, from left to right. Knit them together. One stitch has been decreased.

slip, slip, slip, knit Slip next three stitches knitwise, one at a time, to right-hand needle. Insert tip of left-hand needle into fronts of these stitches, from left to right. Knit them together. Two stitches have been decreased.

slip stitch An unworked stitch made by passing a stitch from the left-hand to the right-hand needle as if to purl.

work even Continue in pattern without increasing or decreasing. (U.K.: work straight)

yarn over Making a new stitch by wrapping the yarn over the right-hand needle. (U.K.: yfwd, yon, yrn)

Embroidery Stitches

French Knot   Straight Stitch

Notes

GET ALL YOUR FAVORITE NICKY EPSTEIN BOOKS AT
SIXTHANDSPRINGBOOKS.COM

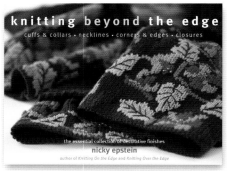

Knitting Beyond the Edge

Knitting Over the Edge

Crocheting On the Edge

Knitting Never Felt Better

Knitting On Top
of the World

Nicky Epstein's
Signature Scarves

Knitting a Kiss in
Every Stitch

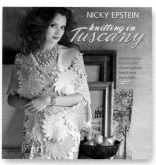

Knitting in Tuscany

Knitted Flowers

Yarn Resource List

ACIAR DEL CIELO
)% Cotton Combed
eight: 50grams / 1.75oz
prox.: 125 meters / 137 yards
edle Size: 3 to 4mm / 5-6 US
uge: 6 to 7 stitches per inch / Sport

ANACO
% Alpaca (Peru) / 40% Merino Wool (Patagonia)
eight: 100grams / 3.5oz
prox.: 133 meters / 145 yards
edle Size: 6 to 7mm / 10 – 10 3/4 US
uge: 3 to 4 stitches per inch Bulky

VERNAL
% Angora Rabbit (Argentina) 25% Merino Wool
tagonia) 25% Poliamyde
eight: 100grams / 3.5oz
prox.: 270 meters / 295 yards
edle Size: 4 to 5mm / 6-8 US
uge: 4 to 5 stitches per inch / Worsted

1A CLASICO
)% Pima Cotton
eight: 50grams / 1.75oz
prox.: 100 meters / 109 yards
edle Size: 4.5mm / 7 US
uge: 5 stitches per inch / Worsted

NTA FE
TTLE HAND DYED COLLECTION
% Merino Wool 15% Polyamide
eight: 50grams / 1.75oz
prox.: 165 meters / 180 yards
edle Size: 3.25mm / 3 US
uge: 6 1/2 to 7 stitches per inch / Sock Fingering

Machine washable in cold water dry flat

LITORAL
50% acrylic 50% polyamide
Weight: 100grams / 3.5 oz
Approx.: 110 meters/ 120 yards
Needle size: 7 a 8 mm/ 10.5 to 11 US
Gauge: 3 stitches per inch / Bulky
Machine washable in cold water dry flat

ARTESANAL
40% Cotton 30% Alpaca (Peru) 30% Polyamide
Weight: 100grams / 3.5oz
Approx.: 200 meters / 218 yards
Needle size: 5 to 6mm / 8-10 US
Gauge: 4 stitches per inch / Heavy Worsted

CLASS
55% Cotton 45% Viscose
Weight: 100grams / 3.5 oz
Approx.: 220 meters / 240 yards
Needle size: 3 1/2 to 4 1/2 mm / 4 to 7 US
Gauge: 5 to 6 stitches per inch / Sport

DEL CERRO
100% Merino Wool (Patagonia)
Weight: 50grams / 1.75oz
Approx.: 115 meters / 127 yards
Needle size: 4 to 5mm / 6-8 US
Gauge: 4 to 5 stitches per inch / Worsted

DEL SUR
100% Merino Wool (Patagonia)
Weight: 100grams / 3.5oz
Approx.: 80 meters / 87 yards
Needle size: 9 to 10mm / 13-15 US

Gauge: 2 to 3 stitches per inch / Super Bulky

BARILOCHE
KETTLE HAND DYED COLLECTION
85% Merino Wool 15% Polyamide
Weight: 100grams / 3.5oz
Approx.: 160 meters / 175 yards
Needle Size: 4.5 to 5mm / 7 to 8 US
Gauge: 4 stitches per inch on US 8 needle /
4 1/2 stitches per inch on US 7 needle / Worsted

LOS ANDES
KETTLE HAND DYED COLLECTION
85% Merino Wool 15% Polyamide
Weight: 100grams / 3.5oz
Approx.: 80 meters / 87 yards
Needle Size: 9 to 10mm / 13-15 US
Gauge: 2 to 3 stitches per inch / Super Bulky

TANGO
90% acrylic 10% polyamide
Weight: 100grams / 3.5 oz
Approx.: 120 meters/131 yards
Needle size: 5 to 6mm / 8 to 10 US
Gauge: 5 to 6 stitches per inch / Worsted / DK
Machine washable in cold water dry flat

ROYAL ALPACA
100% Royal Alpaca
Completely De-haired, 19-19.5 Microns
Weight: 100grams / 3.5oz
Approx: 200 meters/220 yards
Needle size: 4 to 5mm / 6-8 US
Gauge: 5 to 6 stitches per inch / DK
Available in 100% Natural and Dyed Colors

oduced by SOHO Publishing, LLC,, exclusively for AslanTrends.
otographs by Jack Deutsch
xt copyright © 2010 by AslanTrends USA Corp.
otographs copyright © 2010 by AslanTrends USA Corp.

ISBN # 978-0-615-36961-7
1 3 5 7 9 10 8 6 4 2 PRINTED IN USA
FIRST EDITION

Distributed in the USA by:

ASLANTRENDS USA CORP
8 Maple Street # 11
Port Washington, NY, 11050
www.aslantrends.com
contact@aslantrends.com

Unicorn Books & Crafts, Inc.
1338 Ross Street
Petaluma, CA 94954
www.unicornbooks.com
help@unicornbooks.com

Nicky Epstein is a world-renowned knitwear designer, teacher and author of more than 20 best-selling books. Her knitting and crochet books range in subject matter from original reference, historical, travel, and Barbie doll knits to amazingly creative design and pattern books. These must-have titles include the acclaimed "Edgings" series, *Knitting Never Felt Better, Knits for Barbie Doll, Knitting On Top of the World, Knitting in Tuscany, Knitted Embellishments,* and *Crocheted and Knitted Flowers.* She has won the Independent Publisher's Award for Best Craft book three times.

Her innovative, fashionable, whimsical and award-winning designs have appeared in every major knitwear magazine, in museums and on television, and she has taught classes to knitters around the world and hosted many *Vogue Knitting* tours, both local and overseas.

She loves to share her expertise and enthusiasm for knitting with her countless fans, who appreciate her imaginative techniques along with her seemingly fathomless creative designs.

She lives in New York City but travels extensively, bringing her knitting along.

MANY THANKS TO:

Angelo Fernandez, who is from the same town in Spain as my father's family. It was a pleasure working with him and Aslan Trends.

Stu Berg, a long time friend to everyone in our knitting industry.

Jo Brandon, whose help, skill and friendship were invaluable.

Rita Greenfeder, a technical editor and friend.

Nancy Henderson, an amazing knitter and instruction writer.

Eva Wilkin, Eileen Curry, Heris Stenzel, Kristy Lucas, extraordinary knitters who are always there for me.

The Soho Publishing staff who, as a team, can't be beat: **Lisa Buccellato, Loretta Dachman, Sarah DeVita, Sarah Liebowitz, Renee Lorian, Trisha Malcolm, Carla Scott, Kristina Sigler, Lori Steinberg** and **Wendy Williams**.

Jack Deutsch, photographer, and **Joe Vior,** creative director, whose talents captured the essence of this "Enchanting Collection."